Reflexões
de
JP Suassuna

ISBN: 1725910381
ISBN-13: 978-1725910386

Toda honra, toda glória
ao
Senhor JESUS!

Contents

The Healing Power of Sida

This book is written to be an easy read that tells you how to grow Sidas, how to harvest them, and how to make simple medicinals from them. My growing experience is with Sida acuta, but the growing conditions and requirements for Sida cordifolia and Sida rhombifolia are quite similar.

This small book is based on a larger reference book I wrote on the genus Sida. This "big book"* comprises all of the peer-review research on Sidas from around the world, as well as traditional uses for a wide array of health benefits, including Ayurvedic medicine. It is fully referenced. I call it "the physician's desk reference on Sida." I wrote it to give natural healers a trustworthy reference to a medicinal that is "new" to our Western temperate climates.

This **User's Guide** focuses on the three Sidas that you can actually get seeds or starts for: Sida acuta, Sida cordifolia, and Sida rhombifolia. Seeds (with directions) for all three will be available from my website (bbruneau.com) by early May.

Please note: this book is not to be considered medical advice. I strongly advise you to consult your medical provider before trying Sidas for any health benefit.

My wife and I started Bountiful Gardens seeds in 1982. For 33 years we were at the forefront of providing seeds for heirloom vegetable, grain and medicinal plant growers; yet I had never heard of Sida until six years ago when I read Stephen Harrod Buhner's classic, **Herbal Antibiotics: Natural Alternatives for Treating Drug-Resistant Bacteria**.

This book blew my mind simultaneously in three directions:

---

* Sida acuta, Sida cordifolia, Sida rhombifolia, Etc.: Everything Science and Tradition Knows About the World's Best Herbal Antibiotics, Used by Millions of People Every Day, Top Ayurvedic Herbs, Protein-Rich Survival Plants, Superior Fiber, Grow Them with Your Tomatoes   ISBN = 978-0-9748799-3-2
567 pages   809 citations   Price $29.45

First, it scared the living daylights out of me. Buhner provided irrefutable evidence that ALL pharmaceutical antibiotics would be useless in 5-10 years (this was in 2012). He was pronouncing the death of all pharmaceutical antibiotics. My research shows his timeline still seems right in line with current events.

Second, he gave us a possible solution; that there are herbs and shrubs that are powerful enough to replace our failed pharmaceuticals. Standing alone at the top of Buhner's list were three tropical plants: Cryptolepis, Alchornea, and Sida.

Third, one of these top herbal antibiotics in the world (best in my estimation) is a native plant. The genus Sida is an American native born in Mexico and considered a native in our own South. I had been in the rare seed business for 33 years, with a minor specialty of medicinal herbs, and I had never heard of Sida!

Discovering the Power of Sida

I knew immediately that this could be a solution to a mysterious infection that was attacking my otherwise healthy heart. I went online and found what was called a CSA mix – Cryptolepis, Sida, and Alchornea all in equal parts. This extract mix stopped an attack of arrhythmia or afib within minutes!

It did not take long to realize that I was now dependent on wild-crafted herbs from troubled central Africa. Was there any way to replicate these medicinals in Mendocino county without a greenhouse?

Cryptolepis sanguinolenta is a tropical vine, which is harvested for its roots. Alchornea cordifolia is a small tropical tree. I had no way of growing these plants at the time, and they both suggested years until harvest.

Sida, on the other hand, was a small bush, or even ground plant. There was a chance that I could get it through our chilly Winter. Research suggested that 20 degrees Fahrenheit was a killing temperature – we can dip into the teens in the Winter, so nothing was sure.

No Western herbal has Sida in it, most likely because it was "a tropical plant" and therefore assumed to be confined to hot climates or greenhouses. I had no information on Sida aside from Buhner's excellent summary.

I started the seeds in flats in late April, hoping that some might sprout. Our official "safe" planting date in Willits is May 15. I did not treat or "scarify" these seeds (increases your germination). I started the seeds indoors in the even temperature of our rammed earth home; I got almost complete germination! The big question came next: would they survive outside in Willits spring?

When the soil warmed up I transplanted most of these Sidas outside into two small raised beds totaling maybe 100 square feet, hoping that they could survive our cool evenings. I had a bunch of seedlings left over so I put them into several five gallon buckets. All of the seedlings continued to grow! Through the ups and downs of our spring and summer weather the Sidas thrived! (Although they peaked in October, some plants lasted until December.)

They survived every transplanting no matter how botched and brutal. They thrived in the five gallon planters, and subsequently I have had good success with six plants in a three gallon container. These plants will survive and thrive despite being heavily root-bound when grown as annuals.

My favorite Sida transplant story is finding a forgotten six-pack of Sidas horribly overgrown. Pulling them out, all you could really see was a huge mass of roots. So I tore off the bottom third and put it aside for tinctures! I feathered out the remaining roots, planted them into a raised bed, watered well, and that was that. Every transplant I have butchered survived and thrived.

What was particularly exciting was how they thrived in five-gallon buckets and tubs. Planted four or five to a tub they were growing about as well as the beds. Nearly anyone anywhere could grow Sida!

More information on the genus Sida, as well as photos (and links to photos) of the medicinal Sidas are on my website (bbruneau.com).

Using Sida as a Medicinal

Here's how simple it is: Even apartment dwellers with a porch, or any space at all, can grow a bunch of Sidas in a planter, harvest the plant, drown it for a few months in some vodka, and have some potent medicine for when they really need it.

Sidas are some of the most feared weeds in the tropics (and in the near desert as well) but they cannot survive our Mendocino cold wet Winters. Twenty degrees kills them. What they **can** do is become an essential addition to the annual garden.

When my Sidas first began to branch out, I began to harvest the leaves. I did not know much at that point, but most of the research I found used the leaves. I had no idea whether these first-year plants were medicinal, or could be medicinal, but I had to try.

As soon as I had enough leaves saved, I stuffed them into a jar, flooded it with 80 proof vodka, sealed it, and let it sit for six months. When I finally tried it, it was good, not quite as good as the commercial, but I found that increasing my dose 50% equaled the commercial stuff!

This was a huge discovery! Everything I had read assumed that you collected leaves from established perennial plants. That is reasonable when it is growing wild all around you. No one had ever bothered to try growing Sida as an annual for medicinal production. And it is so easy! I have been independent of commercial sida extract since. I now use 70% alcohol for the extracts, which I find completely matches the commercial.

My second thought on reading Buhner's book was, "I love my county and I do not want to see it decimated!" Really! I love my community and the people I live with! I want Sida (and Cryptolepis and Alchornea, and more, eventually) all over my county protecting us against the "untreatable" pathogens that over 70 years of pharmaceutical antibiotics (and antifungals etc.) have bred.

Sidas are not the only solution to our health problems, but they are absolutely the best (and easiest) first step you can make for home-based health. Sidas can protect you against many (if not most) disabling conditions and diseases. Hundreds of millions of people over thousands of years can't be all that wrong. If you already take herbs this will go right to the front of your herb cabinet.

A Powerful Herbal Antibiotic, Antifungal, etc.

• Sidas are consumed by millions of people every day all over the world for a wide array of health problems, and people have been healing themselves with Sidas for thousands of years.

• Sidas control or kill 27 pathogenic bacteria, including many resistant strains, including MRSA.

• Sidas have good effect against malaria and other parasites.

• Sidas have tested well against 16 different pathogenic fungi, including 15 strains of candida.

• Sidas have only been tested against cancer 40 times. Every one of them has had significant benefits; many were cytotoxic, apoptotic, etc. Not one study was followed up.

• Sidas protect your liver, kidney & brain (and more), are blood cleansing and help to balance your fats/lipids. They are adaptogenic, tonic, aphrodisiac, benefit your digestion, etc.

• There are 160 ways that Sida can benefit you.

• Sida acuta can be grown in Zone 8 outdoors. If you can grow tomatoes, you can probably grow Sida.

• This book is completely based on peer-review research, with some expert testimony.

....

For the first time, researchers have found a person in the United States carrying bacteria resistant to antibiotics of last resort, an alarming development that the top U.S. public health official says could mean "the end of the road" for antibiotics. It's the first time this colistin-resistant strain has been found in a person in the United States. In November, public health officials worldwide reacted with alarm when Chinese and British researchers reported finding the colistin-resistant strain in pigs and raw pork and in a small number of people in China. The deadly strain was later discovered in Europe and elsewhere. "It basically shows us that the end of the road isn't very far away for antibiotics — that we may be in a situation where we have patients in our intensive care units, or patients getting urinary-tract infections for which we do not have antibiotics." CDC Director Tom Frieden said in an interview. [The Washington Post, May 27, 2016]

Sidas have shown good effect against something like 65 pathogens including: Staph (18 specific strains of Staph, including MRSA and other multi-drug resistant strains), Candida (including at least 6 resistant strains), some cancers, gonorrhea, typhoid, Aspergillus mold, E. coli, Herpes simplex, Kebsiella (pneumonia and hospital infections), Malaria, Mycobacterium, Salmonella (both food poisoning and typhoid), Shigella (diarrhea and dysentery), Strep (cavities, pneumonia), and intestinal worms.

MRSA (Staph) can be cured by taking ½ teaspoon to a tablespoon of Sida acuta extract 3 to 6 times a day for up to 60 days, according to Buhner. Or steep 2-3 teaspoons of powdered leaves in 6 ounces of hot water for 15 minutes for acute conditions. Drink up to 10 cups a day. The best way to avoid this is to take Sida every day.

There are 160 or so other proven benefits from taking Sida including: adaptogenic, anti-oxidant, analgesic; kidney, liver, heart and brain protective; beneficial for human reproduction; and chemoprotective. It is a mineral accumulator, a fuel source, and it is a host plant for birds, bees, and butterflies, among other things. The Sidas are excellent fiber plants. The leaves have at least 18% good protein (some have over 30%); Sida is considered a survival food.

Every part of a sida plant is anti-pathogenic, in slightly different ways. What I mean by "anti-pathogenic" is that it is not just antibacterial, but also anti-fungal, anti-cancer, and anti-malarial (and similar parasites). Even if you are in perfect health, sidas will help you. They keep your body "tuned up," and your blood and your organs in good health.

How Sidas Stop Pathogens

Nearly every herbalist will tell you that the whole of a plant, as opposed to certain individual constituents, offers additional benefits due to the synergy between the individual elements of the plant. Consider that a plant first and foremost is protecting itself, and that over millennia it has found ways to internally craft great synergies from the natural interactions of its many constituents. Most Western research has been in search of a single compound, a super-star compound, that Western pharmaceutical companies can synthesize, patent, and sell for a ton of money as a sole cure. This compound may or may not even be the same as the original.

Unfortunately, pathogens are actually very, very clever and have become quite adept at finding ways to neutralize any single compound that gets in their way. Buhner describes pharma's complete failure in several very clear and thorough chapters in his book, **Herbal Antibiotics**. I highly recommend that everyone read it now! The time grows short.

There is now a long list of pathogens that are resistant to all antibiotics except colistin, and colistin's end is quite near. Colistin was discontinued as an antibiotic in the 1960s due to its toxic effects on your kidneys, but was reintroduced when all the other antibiotics started to become useless. Bacteria are increasingly resistant to Colistin as well.

When pharmaceutical companies extract individual substances out of the complex that is a plant, and then put them to use killing pathogens, these single compounds are relatively quickly neutralized by those pathogens. So for a short-term gain, the medicinal value from this substance is lessened in the future. This works against its forever value for both the plant and humans.

This backwards way of thinking is what got us into this mess to begin with. Creating more single solutions for the bacteria to quickly neutralize just gets us further and further behind in finding a long-term solution; a solution that is sustainable. The only solutions that are sustainable are, in my opinion, natural complex solutions from natural living plants, solutions that the pathogens never figure out.

Sidas can Help Save Us All

The few studies that have looked at the benefits of consuming a whole Sida plant together are quite encouraging. Last year I realized that in making the tincture only from the leaves I was missing out on additional benefits from the root, stem, bark, seed, fruit, blossom, bud, etc. **All parts of Sida are medicinal** according to the peer-review research, and the different parts are medicinal in at least somewhat different ways.

The Sidas in this book are essentially non-toxic, and highly anti-inflammatory and analgesic. They can be considered a tonic and adaptogenic that keeps the body in good health. Sidas are anti-pathogen (antibiotic, anti-malaria, anti-worm, cytoxic, anti-fungal, and somewhat antiviral). The pathogens have yet to figure out Sida after millions of years.

Sidas are amazing plants. Sida cordifolia is a central nervous system sedative and depressant, but is also a CNS stimulant. Sida acuta is an abortifacieant and an anti-implantation contraceptive that has no lingering effects, but it is also an aphrodisiac and uterotonic. It is essential for post-delivery, and has a long history of helping general female problems like vaginal candidiosis. Sida acuta is also aphrodisiac for men, improves low or no sperm, and is useful for male sexual problems like impotence. I have listed over 160 health benefits that the Sidas deliver – these are but a few.

Since I started this project, there has not been a day passing that I do not feel the urgency to get this information out in a useful form before it is too late. It will take time to spread this information and for us to compound Sida into the most useful herbal anti-pathogens. I am not sure that we will have enough time to avoid or neutralize the multiple epidemics from pathogens fully resistant to all Pharmaceutical antibiotics.

Many Other Health Benefits of Sida

I have been taking Sida acuta extract continuously for six years now and extensive testing by my doctor shows my 71 year old body to be in excellent condition. My lab work is solidly in the green zone.

Sidas are non-toxic and without significant side-effects, with the exception of Sida cordifolia and blood pressure (contains significant ephedrine). Sidas do not interfere with pharmaceutical drugs. Rather, they often amplify pharma's power (can equal them alone).

Ayurveda is the ancient Indian health system that rivals the Chinese in age and effectiveness. Ayurvedic physicians look at your whole lifestyle when figuring out how to keep you healthy. Sidas are some of the premier herbs in Ayurveda, including the legendary Bala.

Sidas are also Rasayana herbs which are adaptogenic and life-enhancing medicine.

While the emphasis is on its medicinal qualities, there is so much more to Sida's health giving qualities! For example, science now recognizes that inflammation is a major source of disease. Sidas are supremely anti-inflammatory and anti-oxidant. They are adaptogenic, allowing your body to adjust to our changing lifestyles. In our polluted world they are chemo-protective and a wonderful detoxicant, especially for your brain.

Sida plants have many non-health benefits as well. One example - young leaves and stems of Sida plants make an excellent natural soap, recommended for tender and irritable skin while helping it heal. Even better, the saponins (which make up the soap) are a complex medicinal in themselves.

Sida As Food

Sida acuta? That poor people food!"

This is what our Ecology Action intern from Haiti said when I told him I was growing Sida acuta. I really like poor people food.

Sidas are an excellent food source, hardy and nutritious enough to be considered survival food. The whole plant can be dried for later medicinal use.

The leaves have excellent protein (18-30+% protein, determined by how well you feed the plant), as well as good protein value in the rest of the plant. Sidas are also chock-full of vitamins and minerals. How about a homemade nutritional powder to add to your shakes, soups, and other edibles?

Sida acuta Protein Score Card

Leaf   18% to 39%
Root   5.7% to 9.4%
Seed   12.6% to 23.2%

What does Sida taste like? I can tell you that fresh Sida acuta leaves are wonderfully tasteless. I make my tea from the combined aerial parts of Sida acuta, and it is nicely tasty. The leaves disappear into soups and stews. The alcoholic tincture (extract) is one of the few that is described as delicious and one that delights the tongue.

Which Sida should you grow?

Sidas are an ideal plant for beginning gardeners. Growing them is very easy, and leaves a lot of room for mistakes. They only need sun, warmth, some water, and lots of fertilizer. They can survive some drought, excessive rain, and very little weeding.

Any of the three Sidas featured in this book will serve you well, and are remarkably similar in most of their medicinal applications. I would recommend growing all three if you can.

Sida acuta is the only Sida to have berberine, a real plus. Sida cordifolia is the legendary Bala of Ayurveda, as well as being the most anti-viral. It is also the most drought hardy. Its heart-shaped leaves give you a bigger harvest of leaves. Sida rhombifolia has unique traditional uses like blood cleaning, is particularly hypoglycemic, and perhaps makes the best fiber (comparable to jute). Its leaves are smoked for a mild euphoria.

I have limited experience starting and growing the other two Sidas, but so far I find Sida acuta easy to germinate (and grow) in our cool mountain climate. All Sidas will willingly hybridize, providing a fertile ground for new localized species of Sida.

Using Sida as a Medicinal

Important things to consider

Some natural medicines require special processing to retain their medicinal value. The medicinals in Sida seem to be very stable and resistant to damage. Cooking is not a problem. The only caveat is to use acid water in any processing – this brings out the most valuable alkaloids. When making tinctures, use acid water (pH 6 or less) as the base. If making a tea, use acidic water. If not using water at all, try to add some acid content (lemon juice, vinegar, etc.)

When I talk about alcohol I am always talking about ethanol, the alcohol in beer, wine, and vodka. Any other alcohol is poison. Wood alcohol, isopropyl alcohol, and so on, are poisonous if swallowed! Be very sure you are using ethanol!

Most research has focused on either the leaves or roots, but enough research has been done to show that all the other parts of Sida (flowers, buds, seeds, fruits, etc) also have medicinal value, often unique medicinal value in some way. All parts of Sida are non-toxic with no known side-effects. I now personally harvest the whole plant (except the stalks which are excellent fiber) and process it all into my medicines.

Fresh – I find the fresh leaves nicely tasteless, but after a few hours they get limp and stringy, but still with an ok taste. It would make a good ingredient in fresh salads. Get your protein, antibiotic, vitamins, and minerals all before the main dish. It also makes a good pot herb any time: put it in soups, stews, or any meal with greens added.

I make my tinctures from fresh herb rather than dried, which is what commercial sources use. There is no data on this but it seems to me that the fresh living plant is the best place to start. I recommend curing your tinctures as long as possible.

Dried – Drying Sida does not seem to diminish its medicinal value and gives you many options. Drying and powdering it gives you an extremely useful base that stores well and is ready to become a tea or tincture, or be consumed directly. Most researchers use dried Sida leaves or roots for their experiments. Traditional users dry the Sida and use it later for food and medicine. Commercial tinctures are made from dried Sida leaves. Most of the world takes a tea of dried Sida leaves.

Growers really can't fail with a Sida crop. If they can't sell it fresh, they can either tincture it right away, or dry it for later use. They have the flexibility to wait for market demand and fill it when it does appear. Of course, in my opinion there will be an overwhelming demand for anything Sida for years to come.

Preparing Simple Medicinals

The benefits of taking whole part plant preparations are numerous. This means that the chemical constituents that are present in the plant occur in their natural proportions rather than in a standardized percentage. Many people believe that taking the whole plant brings with it the naturally occurring "holistic" balance of medicine that nature provides.

Of course nothing in this book is intended to treat any medical condition. What I offer here are traditional uses and results from peer-review research (based on my "big book"). You should always consult your health provider before trying anything in this book.

It is hard to make specific recommendations on quantities and concentrations. I could only find a few experts who make explicit recommendations. The different Sidas, the parts of the Sida plant used, how it is extracted, how long the extraction process took, any of these affect recommendations.

Do not despair! Any way you take Sida is beneficial. Even if your extract is weak, more is better, and the upper limits of intake are pretty high. I describe below how I make alcoholic Sida extracts that work for me.

Both peer-review research and traditional use demonstrate that Sidas have great health effects however you consume them. The one big gotcha is to always use acidic water (pH 6-) as part of your formulation to bring out the essential alkaloids. If water is not part of your formulation, add some lime juice, vinegar or another source of acidity.

Generally Sida formulations are dose dependent, that is, the more you take, the stronger the effect. Different parts of a Sida plant have somewhat different medicinal strengths. There are differences in the effectiveness of water and alcoholic extracts although both are very effective.

There are no reported side-effects from taking Sida in anywhere near-normal amounts, except Sida cordifolia which contains significant ephedrine, a stimulant that requires caution.

Sidas have been documented to actually amplify or increase the effectiveness of pharmaceutical drugs. Sidas have been shown to equal or exceed the effectiveness of standard pharmaceutical antibiotics, antifungals, NSAIDs, etc. (See list at end of book.)

Hot water Sida extracts perform very well in peer-review research. Alcohol extracts also perform very well against other weird and exotic extracts used by scientists. I would say the hot water extract and/or a 40% vodka extract can pretty much do everything a Sida can do – which is quite a lot! Nevertheless, I would always prefer a 60-70% ethanol extract.

Powder

The dried parts of Sida made into a powder can be used as a powder directly on the skin, or consumed for gastro-intestinal tract conditions. Sida powder can be easily used as a tea, can be turned into a tincture, or used as a superior nutritional supplement. While the leaves are commonly used for this because of their high protein content, the whole plant can be powdered and used medicinally.

Sida root powder is traditionally administered orally for pneumonia and intestinal parasites, among other things. It has been traditionally used for skin infections, skin wounds, and dermatitis of various sorts. Sida powders are an Ayurvedic cure for leprosy. Just sprinkle the powder over the affected part as often as needed.

Powders officially last a minimum of 6 months but properly stored can last much longer. If stored in a cool place, away from light, and very dry they should last for years.

Ayurvedic Safe Dosage: Sida acuta 2-4 grams, S. cordifolia 1-3 grams, S. rhombifolia 3-6 grams, probably the root/leaf powder (I personally would use a touch more of the whole plant powder). I would try to limit my total dosage for a day to 12 grams.

Tea / Decoction

Probably 100 million people in the tropics take Sida as a tea of the powdered dried leaves and/or roots. Leaves and roots act about the same way. I prefer to include the whole plant in my extracts.

Dosage: Buhner recommends 1-2 teaspoons of powdered leaves in 6 ounces of water. Steep for 15 minutes. As a preventative: 1-2 cups a day. In acute conditions: up to 10 cups a day. As eye drops: 1-3 drops as needed, 3-6 times a day.

A general recommendation for any herb tea is two teaspoons in a cup of water in a slow boil of 10-30 minutes.

Ayurvedic Pharmacopoeia As a tea 3-6 gm of powder of S. cordifolia is recommended. The Quality Standards of Indian medicinal Plants have also mentioned 3-6 gm as safe dose. A large dose is 10 grams of Sida cordifolia per cup of water that has been steeped for at least one hour and taken by mouth as tea. The dose of S. rhombifolia is 3-6 gm. Traditionally 2-4 gm is considered as safe dose of S. acuta tea.

Scientist's strong dosage: Researchers use one part of powdered root of Sida rhombifolia and four parts of acidic (pH 6-) water and boiled for 15 minutes. Various studies have used 100 grams (about 4 ounces) of powdered Sida leaves boiled in quart of water (hopefully acidic) for 3 hours or more.

Tincture / Extract

When a plant is processed to remove bulk and retain the active phytochemical constituents from the plant matter, the resulting substance is called an extract. This means that the bulk matter is greatly reduced and what remains is more condensed; so a smaller quantity can be taken medicinally.

Preparing a tincture: The general recommendation is to chop up the herbs finely, then soak them in 65% ethanol extract for 4-6 weeks, shaking daily. My first batch of Sida acuta leaves was made with 40% vodka. I did not chop up the leaves and did not shake the jar more than a few times, but I let it sit for 6 months. It had 66% of the strength of the commercial extracts! A dose and a half equaled them. Now I use 70% tinctures and let them soak for at least a year. I am currently using my last year's harvest.

I have tinctures dating back to 2014 which I plan to test somehow someday. I have never heard anyone limit how long an extract can be left to soak or how long it remains medicinal.

How I made my tincture: I wait until I have enough Sida material to stuff a jar full. It can be a small jar. If I am using all aerial parts and roots, I make sure that they are chopped enough to pack easily. I pack the jar until it is full and resists adding more material. The packed material should resist when lightly pushed.

I then fill the jar with alcohol. 40% (80 proof) vodka makes an ok Sida extract. 70% alcohol makes a much better extract. I buy a gallon of organic 100% alcohol (go online and search for: "where to buy pure ethanol"). I mix equal parts of vodka and 100% alcohol which yeilds 2 parts of 70% alcohol. Be absolutely sure you are buying ethanol (vodka, etc) – any other alcohol is poison!

The alcohol level can drop as the plant breaks down and occupies less room. Be sure the alcohol level is always above all the herb. Check on the level of your extracts, daily at first, and then weekly for a couple of months. Leaving herb exposed can cause you to lose the whole batch to mildew or rot. Maintain an inch of alcohol above the herbs to be sure.

Dosage: Stephen Buhner in his book **Herbal Antibiotics** recommends a general daily dose of a 1:5 tincture (one part alcohol to five parts herb) with 60% alcohol. 20 to 40 drops up to four times daily. For MRSA and the like: ½ teaspoon to one tablespoon, 3-6 times a day, for up to 60 days.

I personally take four standard droppers-full once a day, and I have been doing this for six years. That is about 250 drops. I like to take one large dose a day because Sidas actions are "dose dependent", that is, the more you use the better the result. I am pretty sure that Sida stays in your system at least 36 hours, so I get the benefit of one strong dose while having good coverage all the time. I would not hesitate to use more if I thought it might help.

Interesting note: In one study, when Sida acuta extract was tested against some bacteria, researchers found the freshly prepared extract had no effect. On the other hand, extracts stored for 21 days had a significant effect with a large "kill zone".

Shelf life: at least one year. I know of no study that actually puts an age limit on tinctures If you keep it well sealed against air, cool and completely out of the light, the industry says shelf life can be up to 4 years. I would say longer than that.

Sida Cultivation Narrative

If you like tables and lists, the **Sida Cultivation Tables** (which follow this narrative) provide a long list of cultivation topics on each of the Sidas, such as Habitat, Zone (USDA), pH (soil), Sun , etc.

What I present here is a cultivation narrative based on my experience of growing Sida for five years, and turning the harvest into a powerful medicinal. What I have been growing is Sida acuta, but cultivation (and medicinal effects) for all three are essentially the same. The second edition of this small introduction will have more detailed information on any differences.

Growing Environment

All three Sidas are considered weeds in the tropics, and a danger to commercial plantings there. Sidas have spread from tropical Mexico to cover the tropical and sub-tropical worlds: Tropical America, Africa, India, SE Asia, Australia, Oceana, our Caribbean, and our own tropical South. These are tough survival plants once you get them started. Sidas compete vigorously with other plant species.

Perennial Sidas have a deep taproot and can withstand drought, mowing and shallow tillage. They are weeds of degraded pastures, tree plantations, cereals, root crops, vegetables, planted forests, lawns, roadsides, and waste places. In warm climates these are weeds that can inspire fear (unless you avidly harvest them for their medicinal content).

Sidas are ubiquitous in the tropics, so if you live in a tropical or sub-tropical climate you might look around your neighborhood and see if you do not already have them volunteering. If you are a gardener in the temperate zone (most of the US) then things get a little more complicated. If your soil is warm enough (60 degrees F) for at least three months you can probably have a good enough harvest to be useful. Generally, if you can grow tomatoes you can probably grow Sida.

Sidas should do fine in just about any soil you put them in. They are found on most soil types, except seasonally flooded clays or soils derived from limestone. They do not like soil with lime in it: limestone, serpentine soils, lime added to the soil, are all no-nos.

People add lime to make the soil less acid. Do not do this to Sida, it will greatly damage its growth. Sidas can do well in soils with clay as long as they drain well, but any amount of clay makes cleaning the roots a much bigger chore later.

Sida seeds will not grow in soil that is cooler than 60 degrees. Once they are growing well and somewhat mature Sida acuta can withstand occasional light freezes and temperatures down to freezing at least. Nevertheless, Sidas will start to die, and their leaf growth will be less, when things start to get cold.

They grow in tropical Africa, so they can take heat and humidity. Despite being a tropical plant Sidas aren't fussy about air humidity levels; all three species in this book survive on the fringes of the Sahara Desert! Sida acuta and Sida rhombifolia have also been found in Antarctica! They can take a reasonable amount of drought as well, but it is best to keep them watered.

When growing, Sidas prefer direct sunlight, although they'll also grow in a fair amount of shade. But direct sunlight will give better conditions, which will result in bigger, healthier plants and a higher medicinal content. Sidas can grow in significant shade, but you will get your best crop when grown in full sun.

Experiments have demonstrated that Sidas are indifferent to fertilization as far as growth. Fertilized and unfertilized Sidas grow the same, but fertilization is needed for medicinal content.

We had hundreds of Sida sprouts in soil that had no measurable nitrogen. That said, if you want **medicinal** Sida you had better fertilize well. The soil can be poor but if it is well-fertilized you will have a good medicinal crop. My beds seem to like 12-12-12 organic guano, and 10-10-10 is a commercial recommendation. I fertilize well once at the beginning of the season and that is all I fertilize.

I would recommend inter-cropping (growing another crop) in the Sida beds, at least at first to shade the soil. Sidas get along with other plants, that is they do not poison them, but simply out-compete them. Medicinal calendulas as an inter-crop were too large and aggressive. If you like purslane it will grow fast in the beds and is easily harvested when it gets too large. A cover crop like Dutch White clover might be best: it is low-growing, adds nitrogen to the soil, and covers and protects the exposed soil.

Starting From Seed

In early May of 2017 I was worried. I had hypothesized that my Sidas would re-sprout from fallen seed but there were no sprouts. I planted several flats of Sida seed to assure myself of a crop. In late May my wife came in and said, "You have got to look at your Sida bed!" As she was removing the Winter ground cover she discovered hundreds of sprouts! More like 400 sprouts in a 50-square-foot bed. That is wonderful news! That could allow us to multiply Sida out for my whole county in two years if enthusiastically embraced. At the same time all the Sidas came up in the flats. I did not know where to put all of them.

These Sidas had sprouted despite having completely exhausted the nitrogen from both beds in the previous growing season. So I dug up all the Sida sprouts and put them in any available container I could find, flats, quart containers, six-packs, even a cardboard box.

I replaced the top foot of soil in both Sida beds with good quality manufactured organic soil. Still far from ideal, but closer to good garden soil. I added a generous dose of organic 12-12-12 with a liberal dose of kelp meal. Then replanted the best 100 plants to one foot centers. Other sprouts went into some five-gallon cans (four to a three gallon can).

After all of that there still were still 200+ starts, so they got jammed into the end of a bed, maybe 25 square feet, which I called "the jungle." The spacing was from a bunch planted together to one inch. I wanted to observe the dynamics of really close planting. Despite massive overplanting I have not noticed any dead plants in the jungle. Months later all the plants were still there, many with their growth retarded, but all still reaching for the sky, all healthy. They were much smaller in size, a much paler green, few side branches due to the crowding, resulting in completely vertical Sidas.

The best way to have plants next year is to let them go to seed and they will re-sprout in the same bed when the soil gets warm enough. Even if you are vigorously collecting seed, the plant will find ways to drop seed. The only other thing you will need is ground cover. The seed has to be in very shallow soil, or right on top, to germinate. This leaves it exposed to things that would like a tasty nutritious seed. Last year the bed that did not have ground cover, but was the better soil, had virtually no sprouts; while the other bed, with worse soil but ground cover, had all the sprouts!

If you are starting from saved seed, immerse the seed in boiling water for 20 seconds, and then plant immediately, very shallowly, barely covering the seed. I have 100 per cent germination doing this method. Plants started from seed will pause after emergence for a period of weeks before continuing on their growth, so don't fret. Seed that was 3 years old was useless. It was very very slow to develop, and never grew more than a few inches all season.

Sida sprouts are very thin and prone to damage when young. After they've reached a good size, say over 2 inches in height, with at least 2 sets of leaves, they can be separated from each other. I have not had any problems with transplanting Sidas.

Maintenance and Growth

After preparing the soil, I do not add subsequent fertilizer. Betsy faithfully waters once a day, twice on hot days. I left a six pack of Sidas for five days in the office without watering and they were fine.

The leaves are a known treat for deer, which browse it heavily in the wild. Once it gets some size this plant can survive a lot of harvesting. I harvest leaves and seeds every week or two once established.

I seldom weed my Sida beds. Purslane was a good second crop in the Sida beds. It is prolific in early Spring, when the soil is most exposed, and is easily harvested when it starts to take over. Medicinal calendula outgrows the Sida and would certainly impact the harvest. A low-growing ground cover would work well.

Fertilization

An herb like rosemary I would stress for better medicinal production. Sidas are the opposite - feed them well for medicinal production. There is evidence of improved growth with fertilization, but equal evidence that fertilization makes no difference in growth! I found that applying 12-12-12 fertilizer to Sida acuta made no difference in growth or lushness. There is ample evidence that they are essentially indifferent to fertilizer in terms of growth. Sidas do like nitrogen and that does seem to improve size; yet early this year Sidas sprouted and were growing in a bed that had been stripped of nitrogen the growing season before.

Some preliminary studies confirm: fertilize well for good medicinal content. Commercial growers stress feeding well for the best protein and nutrients. I have not had very good soils and have used varied amounts of fertilizer used over the years, yet all my Sida acuta crops have produced an adequate medicinal crop for my needs with a strong annual dose of strong organic fertilizer.

Harvesting Sida Acuta

Weekly Harvesting

I like to let my Sidas get to the branching stage before picking leaves; then I harvest leaves and seeds every week or two throughout the growing season. Deer forage it heavily in our South, so it can take some serious picking.

When Sida acuta (at least) starts to produce seed, it also produces some comparatively large leaves; I call them the "come browse me" leaves because they are right next to seed pods. I think Sida produces these leaves to get the deer to browse the plant, disturb the seed pods, get seed in its fur, and spread the seed. I prefer to pick those big leaves, since that replicates browsing, and they give me a lot more leaf to work with. So I harvest the big leaves and then thin the remaining leaves. I probably take only about 10% of the leaves at a time, but could probably take much more. I find it efficient to harvest the seeds separately.

Final Harvest

Basically you can use the whole plant. Researchers use the leaves or roots for most of their studies, but there is ample evidence that the whole plant is medicinal, and that the different plant parts all have special medicinal qualities or strengths. At first I only used the leaves but then realized I was losing medicinal qualities by not using the other Sida parts. Since last year I have been processing the whole plant for medicinal use.

Here is how I process whole Sida plants. Loosen the soil and carefully dig them up to preserve as much root as possible. I then separate the roots from the aerial parts for later processing since they are hard to clean (use wire cutters to separate; scissors do not work). I will brush or wash off soil attached to the roots, and then put them aside for final cleaning and processing.

The aerial parts have a whole variety of forms from a single un-branched stalk (close planting) to a tangled, spreading multi-branched plant. Since I now value all the aerial parts, harvesting has become easier, I harvest everything. Tangled multi-branched plants are too large, so I cut off all the side branches for individual processing (use wire cutters; scissors do not work).

I put on old nitrile gloves – as they age they harden which is better for stripping stalks. I pinch the top of the stalk firmly between my thumb and forefinger and strip everything downwards – leaves, flowers, buds, seeds, bark – everything is medicinal. If I get some bark, that is great; bark has its own special benefits. Sometimes I can just strip a single-stalked plant once straight down. Other times you have to work your way down the stalk. With all that done there will still be tufts of goodies along the stem and at the top for harvesting. Each plant demands particular attention.

Like everything Sida there is a great variation in roots. Bare roots with few root hairs are easy to clean in a bucket of water. Roots with whole tangles of root hairs are a real pain. They grab onto everything, so if your soil is rocky you will be peeling off a lot of pebbles. If your soil has clay, you will have resistant blobs of clay/root hairs that wetting only makes worse – so I recommend that you avoid clay. Once the roots are dry, crush the soil blobs away, and then wash in water. The main roots should be a creamy yellow/brown with brown filaments.

N.B. If you are processing dried Sida parts, I would recommend a mask and maybe even eye protection, and process with a wind current or a fan. The dry dust that is created by cutting and chopping Sida can be very irritating.

Harvesting Seed

The fruit is shaped like a tiny naval orange, but where the navel is, it begins to open up and peel back as it matures. When the fruit dries out it turns brown and finally almost black. Once brown the seed pod will generally be open enough to harvest the seeds. When black it will drop seed with the lightest touch (unless moist).

To harvest seed I position my fingers over the seed pod and pinch it between my thumb and forefinger. If it is truly ripe it will crumble to my touch and I have the seeds caught between my fingers. If it does not crumble under a strong pinch, then it is not ripe enough no matter how it looks. If you do not pinch the seeds firmly, they will crumble and scatter and you will lose seeds. The seeds do have a sharp short point which you generally avoid by pinching it this way, but if you have sensitive fingers, it is best to wear gloves.

Another method is to carry a wide-mouth jar in one hand, and with the other hand dip a seed cluster into the jar, and roughly rub the cluster of ripe and unripe seed pods. The ripe seed clusters will break apart, and you will get most of the seeds. The unripe pods will resist your efforts; they are hard to separate from the branches.

This is a tropical plant, so just keep the seeds cool and dry. Seed saved at room temperature should be good for two years. Research has shown that properly saved seed can be viable for many years.

Sida Cultivation Tables

Sida acuta

Sida acuta var. carpinfolia, broomweed, wireweed, Common Fanpetals, Bala, Brihannagabala, Rajabala

Description

A small, erect, perennial shrub, branching profusely from the base. It usually ranges from 1-2 feet in height. The stems are fibrous to almost woody, with a tough stringy bark. There is a deep, tough taproot. The leaves are alternate, lanceolate, acute, tapering towards both ends, and on a short, hairy petiole 3-6 mm long.

The leaves have toothed margins, are smooth or have sparse stellate hairs and have prominent veins on the undersurface. The leaves are quite variable in size, from 2-9 cm long and 0.5-4 cm wide. The pair of stipules at the base of each leaf are not equal, with one frequently much narrower than the other.

The flowers are yellow, solitary, 1-2 cm in diameter and on a short stalk 0.3-0.8 cm long. There are five petals, joined at the base and with a shallow notch at the apex. The fruit is a hard, brown capsule, 3-5 mm in diameter, breaking into 5-8 triangular segments. Each segment contains one seed and has a pair of sharp awns or 'beaks' 1-1.5 mm long which attach readily to animal fur or clothing. The seeds are small, reddish-brown to black, wedge-shaped, deeply indented on both sides, rounded on the back and about 1.5 mm long.

Habitat   All tropics and sub-tropics. A major plant in the sub-Saharan Sahel. Grows from sea level to 5,000 feet. Has been found in Antarctica!

Zone (USDA)   8a

pH (soil)   5.0 to 8.0. Weak acid soils ok

Sun Exposure   Sun to partial shade. Will produce more in the sun.

Growth Habit   Small, erect, much branched, perennial shrub

Plant Height   Generally up to 2 feet. Close planting forces 5' stalks.

Soil Environment   Most soil types, except seasonally flooded clays or soils derived from limestone. I would be cautious about much clay in your soil since it is so hard to clean from the roots. Soil should be well-drained and well-fertilized. Sida acuta can survive on pretty bad soil but if you want a good harvest give it the best soil possible.

Soil Temperature for Seed Germination   night time temp. above 60°

How Propagated   Usually by seed. Can also take stem cuttings.

Seed Germ % Purchasing commercial seed from Belize I got irregular germination but otherwise good growth. Subsequent commercial seed that I obtained was coated with a fungicide, and I got close to 100% germination. Using the seeds I grew, dipping them into boiling water for 20 seconds just before planting, gave me 100% germination. The Sida plants volunteering from seed dropped last year must have had good germ, since I had hundreds of sprouts.

Seed Longevity   {no data. In my experience 1-2 years} I have germinated two-year-old S. acuta seed 100% by dipping it in boiling water for 20 seconds and planting immediately. Older seed does not sprout/grow well after two years unless it has been properly dried and frozen

Seed Dormancy   The germination difficulties seem to come up when someone wants Sida to sprout at some other time than the next growing season (in the US that is next Spring when the soil warms up.) Sida is very stubborn about when it wants to sprout.

Seeds per Gram   400 seeds   **[359]**

Seed Depth   0-1/2". Best to surface plant or lightly cover with soil.

Plant Spacing   The literature says 12-15" centers for perennial planting. If you do this add a cover crop to help shade the ground. I prefer 8-10" centers for bushy growth. If you want vertical growth (best fiber) then plant on 1-2" centers. I do not agree with the literature – I think closer spacing gives about as much harvest and keeps any weeds to a minimum. **Containers:** up to 5 plants to a 3 gallon tub, up to 10 plants in a 5 gallon tub.

Germination/Light   Needs light to germinate so plant shallowly. Prefers sunny location but a slightly higher % of seedlings emerge in shade **[306]**

Water Need   Tolerates dry as well as high rainfall conditions. Significantly better growth with daily watering. Consider watering twice on really hot, dry days.

Fertilization   Had significantly increased plant height, size of leaves and higher biomass (and medicinal content) under high soil fertility. Recommend one lb. 10-10-10 fertilizer per 100 sq. ft. (or more) every crop. Last year I added a foot of moderately fertile manufactured soil, and fertilized with a generous dose of organic 12-12-12 with some kelp meal.

Harvest   Weekly - My approach has been to begin harvesting leaves when the plant begins to sprout side branches. There usually are a few very large leaves; I call them the "come browse me" leaves.

I always pick those. And then any old looking leaves. After that maybe do a little general thinning. This plant is made for heavy browsing so you could pick aggressively. **End of Season** – Carefully dig up the whole plant. Clip off the roots. Strip all the aerial parts from the stalks. Commercial growers only use the leaves or roots. I use everything in my tinctures.

Seed Harvest   I harvest the seed when the seed capsule turns dark brown to black and opens. I carefully pinch the seed pod and it crumbles the seed into my pinched fingers. If it doesn't then the seeds are not ready. Hold it too loosely and you will lose the seed.

Another method that works for me is to take a deep bottle and push a cluster of Sida seed capsules into it and roughly rub them all with your fingers. The ripe seed will mostly fall into the container, while the green seed is pretty resistant to picking.

The seeds have sharp point so be careful – you might want to consider gloves. I find it best to harvest the seeds separately. The seed pods when wet do not as easily come apart.

As a Weed   If it can become a serious weed if perennial. As an annual it could possibly spread enough to be considered a weed. I personally would welcome any annual growth as additional harvest.

Butterflies, Bees, Birds Host   Among the best bee plants in Nigeria, and is a high-quality pollen plant. Bees are always around Sida but I have never actually seen them collecting pollen. It could be that they have never experienced Sida and are cautious.
Considered a good host for butterflies. Sharp pointed seeds discourage bird foraging. Domestic Sidas are a major food source for some North American birds. Honey bees require ten essential amino acids, six out of which are present in the pollen of these Sidas, plus some non-essential amino acids. The pollen protein content is also nutritionally important.

....

It is concluded that alcoholic extract of Bala at a dose of 400 mg/kg has potency to act as anti diabetic, hypoglycemic and anti oxidant properties and also helps to check muscle wasting. Further it also protects from LPO that damages the cell membrane (All three Sidas in this book qualify as Bala).... Had bacteriocidal and baceriostatic effect on all bacteria - these effects were stronger in all cases than the control (Cotrimoxazol).

Sida cordifolia

Abutilon ramosum, Country Mallow, Flannel weed, Mahabala

Description

Erect, branched sub-shrubs to 1.5 m tall; stem green, densely tomentose with minute stellate and spreading simple hairs. Leaves 1.5-5.5 x 1-3.5 cm, ovate, rarely suborbicular, base cordate, margins serrate to the base, apex subobtuse or acute, basally 3-5 nerved, densely stellate-tomentose beneath with simple hairs on nerves and soft tomentose above; petiole to 3.5 cm long, pubescent; solitary or aggregated terminally in to congested corymbiform inflorescence; pedicel to 3 mm long in flower, to 1.2 cm in fruits, articulated above the middle.

Calyx 6-7 mm long, prominently 10-ribbed, densely tomentose without. Corolla c. 1 cm across, yellow; petals to 8 x 6 mm, obliquely obovate, apex truncate or slightly emarginate. Staminal column c. 3 mm long. Ovary subglobose, pubescent; styles 8-10; stigma capitate, yellow. Schizocarp 6-7 mm diam., pubescent towards apex; mericarps 8-10, to 3 x 2 mm, trigonous with acute angles, apically 2-awned. Seeds brownish or black.

Habitat   Seems to prefer drier sandy locations, especially near sea-level, but exhibits great range in habitat. Prefers full sun exposure for higher yield of root and medicinals.

Grows throughout India, known for its hot humid summers, but is also a major plant in the sub-Saharan Sahel which is dry 9-10 months a year, with 20" of rain, and poor soil. Does not like cold weather.

Zone (USDA zone)   8a: to -12.2 °C (10 °F) I would say not below 20 deg

pH (soil acidity)   Weak acid soils ok. Less tolerant of more acidic soils

Sun Exposure   Full sun to partial shade. Full sun for higher root yield and medicinal content

Growth Habit   Small, erect, downy shrub [118]

Plant Height   In tropical and temperate climates can grow up to 2 meters. In the sub-Saharan Sahel it grows 3-12"

Soil Environment

Beds   Most soil types, except seasonally flooded clays or soils derived from limestone. I would be cautious about much clay in your soil since it is so hard to clean from the roots. Soil should be well-drained and well-fertilized. For best medicinal production add 1 part soil and 2 parts humus to make a well-drained loam that should remain relatively moist. Can survive long periods of drought. Benefits from the addition of compost.

Pots   Perlite can be added to a commercial potting mix for a suitable medium for growing in containers. One source says plant the seeds in a well drained mix such as 3 parts perlite to 1 part sterile potting soil. I personally find any loose, well-drained soil is fine for Sida acuta. The other two Sidas may need more lightness to their soil and better drainage to be successful in pots.

Soil Temperature for Seed Germ   Sida seeds germinate when night-time soil temperatures are around 60° F. or better

How Propagated   Direct sow or transplant after last frost. Can be grown both from the seeds and by stem cuttings. Start seeds in warm potting soil, or sow directly into the soil when warm enough. You can also take stem cuttings, which flower earlier than seed. Propagation is also reported from tissue culture practices.

Seed Germ Percentage   The literature says boiling and freezing pre-treatments achieved a 50% germination rate. Another source says best germination procedure for Sida cordifolia=12 hr. Refrigerator (45° F) and 12 hr. oven (100° F)= 69% germination in 20 days. The maximum germination percentage is at 100° F. Longer in oven and the percentage germination becomes very low. There is no germination at 140° C.

We are trying the method we use with Sida acuta (which gets us 100% germination): submerge the seed in boiling water for 20 seconds and then plant immediately. Germination has been spotty.

Seed Longevity   Seeds stored at 39° F and 10% humidity retained some viability for 2 years. The seeds of Sida cordifolia have a viability period of 21 months. Professionally preserved seed - 4% germ after 41 years storage in paper bags at room temp.

Seed Dormancy   Germination time is erratic without pre-treatment (see Seed Germ Percentage above) and can take from 10 days to 3 months. Kew Gardens gives germination time of 3 to 8 months. Germination rates are also extremely variable.

Seeds per Gram   110-250

Seed Depth   Surface sown. Sow on surface and lightly cover with soil.

Plant Spacing   15-24 inches (Growing wild in the extremely dry Sub-Sahara zone in Africa, the density ranges from 8 to 183 plants per square meter.)

Germination/Light Protection from light increases germination; seeds lightly buried in the ground and protected from light increase their growth potential and their germination rate.   Can be germinated in full sun only if adequate soil moisture is maintained

Water Need   Plenty of water is not required for its cultivation. Drought-tolerant; suitable for xeriscaping, Water during hot season - regularly but without excess, especially during summer's heat. The soil should remain relatively moist. Wild, it survives on 20 inches of rain a year in the Sahel.

Fertilization   Apply any organic fertilizer. Fertilize regularly during growth but with spacing. Has significantly increased plant height, size of leaves and higher biomass (and medicinal content) with high soil fertility. Recommend one lb. 10-10-10 fertilizer per 100 sq. ft. (or more) every crop. Benefits from added compost and manure. Takes well to green manuring.

Crop Cultivation   Experts say weed the crop at intervals of 20-30 days. Considering that the crop should be harvested at 240 days, I personally think 2-3 weedings and hoeings will, in temperate climates, be more than adequate .

Harvest   Harvest (specifically) at 8 months. My approach has been to begin harvesting leaves when the plant begins to sprout side branches. Initially just do a little general thinning. This plant is made for heavy browsing so you could pick aggressively once fully established. Fresh use of Sida cordifolia as a medicinal plant is most common but drying and subsequent storage before use is practiced as well.

"The fresh root yield at eight months of age was nearly seventy per cent higher than that at nine months of age... The result indicated an increase in dry root yield up to eight months of age and after that a decline was noticed.... The ephedrine content also followed the same trend and was found to be maximum at eight months of age."

Effect of harvesting stage of Sida cordifolia on ephedrine content and ephedrine yield. Grown in full sun

Harvest at:	Fresh root yield (kg ha-1)	Ephedrine yield (%)
6 months	594	0.0006
7 months	1199	0.0045
8 months	1528	0.2859
9 months	899	0.0879
10 months	814	0.0238

(Journal of Tropical Agriculture 53 (1) : 42-47, 2015: "Variation in root yield and ephedrine content of Bala (Sida cordifolia Linn.) at differential harvesting under open and shaded situations")

Be sure to cut up roots while fresh. Dried roots are much more difficult to deal with (and dangerous due to shrapnel). Even for fresh roots you will need a wire clipper.

If you want to grow it as a perennial, you should only cut some side branches and leaves off. Just leave the plant enough leaves to survive the winter, so about 40-50% of it should be left undisturbed.

Its large heart shaped leaves make an awesome stir-fry vegetable... In India Sida cordifolia is cultivated as a high-quality fiber plant. The fiber can be extracted by retting the stem in water.

As a Weed   Considered an invasive weed in Africa, Australia, the southern United States, Hawaiian Islands, New Guinea, French Polynesia, etc..   This is a plant that is considered a nuisance for crop production and on pastureland (feared in Sub-Sahara by the local people due to its rapid expansion - plant density varied between 8-183 plants per square meter)

These plants have a very strong and deep taproot, it can be almost impossible to uproot a plant after its second year. Self-sows freely; deadhead if you do not want volunteer seedlings next season.

Host For Butterflies, Bees, Birds   Attractive to all three. Important pollen source and much more. Attracts bees, wasps and butterflies to its flowers as soon as they are open in the morning. The bees use them as principal pollen source while wasps and butterflies use them as nectar. Potential pollen and nectar sources for honey bees. In Africa honey bees collect Sida pollen voraciously and deposit it in their hives. Ceratina bees, small carpenter bees, also gather pollen for use in brood development. Honey bees require ten essential amino acids, six out of which are present in the pollen of these Sidas, plus some non-essential amino acids. The pollen protein content is also nutritionally important.

....

Bala normalizes vata and sooths excited nerves. For this reason the oil prepared using this herb is used to massage patients who suffer from paralysis, cervical spondylosis, facial paralysis etc. Bala controls motility of large intestine. It helps to absorb water and nutrients from intestines. Hence its preparations are widely used in Grahani or Irritable Bowel Syndrome (IBS). This herb is a very good cardiac tonic and reduces petechial hemorrhage... Because of this property bala is used in ayurvedic preparations which increase sperm count and sperm motility. It helps to increase quality and quantity of semen. This herb is mainly used in male and female infertility. Texts of ayurveda praise the herb Bala as Vrishya (aphrodisiac). Hence this herb is used in conditions like erectile dysfunction and premature ejaculation. The herbal preparations which are used in Female infertility contain this herb as main ingredient as it acts as a very good uterine tonic. Hence it is widely used in convalescing patients as it supplies essential nutrients. It helps to build a healthy body and strengthens body immune system. (All three Sidas in this book qualify as Bala)

Sida rhombifolia

arrowleaf sida, Cuban jute, Bala, Mahabala, Atibala

Description

The stem is erect, branching and covered densely with stellate (star shaped) hairs and is rather twiggy with tough stringy bark. The stem becomes glabrous (without hair or scales) as it approaches the top. The leaves are dull green and lanceolate to linear-oblong sometimes rhombic, alternate and 1.5-8cm long, with serrate margins and finely stellate hairs on the upper surface of the leaf and a dense amount of stellate hairs on the undersurface, making that surface look white. The flowers are small, solitary, pale orange to yellow on slender jointed peduncles (stalks) about 10-30mm long. The peduncles are mostly axillary (formed in the angle between the stems) but sometimes there are clustered of 3 or 4 at the end of branches.

The calyx (collectively the sepals of one flower) is a 5-lobed, 10 ribbed ashy green color with stellate (star shaped) hairs. The corolla (the petals collectively) is 7-8mm long and consists of 5 petals that are united at the base.

The fruit (schizocarp) is 5-6mm in diameter, glabrous (without hair or scales), a dark brown color, more or less globular and vertically ribbed. It is divided into 9-12 fruitlets (mericarps) acting as seeds. In the fruit, the mericarps (fruitlets) are hard and often indehiscent (not opening to release the seed) with a wide back and honeycombed or reticulate sides. The mericarps have 2 erect minutely barbed awns.

Habitat   Commonly found in dry countries. prefers light to medium, well drained soils in an open, sunny position, but is drought and frost tender.

Zone (USDA zone) 9a: to -6.6 °C (20 °F)

pH (soil acidity)   5.0 to 8.0 resulted in 75% germination.

Sun Exposure   In an open, sunny position

Growth Habit   Evergreen shrub. Stem is erect and branching

Plant Height   24-36" Tropics: height of 2m with a spread of 2m.

Soil Environment   Prefers light to medium, well-drained soils in an open, sunny position. Or start in moist but well-drained seed mix. Easily metamorphoses into different varieties, and adapts to different conditions of the soil and other environmental conditions.

Soil Temp for Seed Germ   95° F (35°C) optimum, 68-86°F (20-30° C) ok, 104F° (40° C) no germination.

How Propagated   By seeds or cuttings.

Seed Germ Percentage   62% by hot water pretreatment. Germination was 8% at a temperature of 95°F and was increased to 62% by a hot water (180°F) pretreatment of 10 minutes followed by a cold water (41°F) pretreatment of 10 minutes. Treatment of seed by soaking for 25 minutes in H2SO4 resulted in a germination of 100%. Finally there was 84 % viability after drying to 15% relative humidity and then freezing for 9 weeks.

The emergence of Sida rhombifolia seedlings in pots reached only 35.25% after 40 days of observation. Homeopathic dilutions of Cymbopogon winterianus (citronella) improved germination and growth of seedlings of Sida rhombifolia.

Seed Longevity   Oldest collection 17 years; 96 to 99% germination

Seed Dormancy   Majority dormant 12—24 months after maturity. See Seed Germ Percentage above for details

Seeds per Gram   428

Seed Depth   ½ to 1 1/2 inches (1-4 cm.)
Seedling emergence was greater than 60% at burial depths of ¼-3/4 inches (0.5 -2 cm), but decreased thereafter, and no seedlings emerged from depths exceeding 5.0 cm.

Predators and pathogens were responsible for the loss of 40% of the seeds during the first year of the experiment. The importance of predation declined with depth. Seedling emergence and death are highly dependent on depth of burial.

Plant Spacing   24-36 in (60-90 cm.)

Germination/Light   Light did not influence germination. One study found that seeds buried in the ground and protected from light increased their potential and their germination rate over time.

Water Need   Drought tender. Well drained soils

Fertilization The density was actually higher in the non-fertilized area, but there was no difference in dry matter accumulation between areas. Nevertheless fertilize well for medicinal production. Homeopathic dilutions of Cymbopogon winterianus (citronella) improved germination and growth of seedlings

Harvest   Start harvesting the leaves when side branches appear. Expect 4.5—5 months from weed transplantation or emergence to plant harvest. Medicinal content was not much until 8 months. Leaves are a dried and stored vegetable in S Africa. For fiber production the stems are left to dry for 10—12 days followed by retting in water for another 20 days.

As a Weed   Among the most prominent weeds at all levels of fertilization. S. rhombifolia   grew better and competed better without fertilization. Once established (2-3 years) control by hand pulling and mowing are only partially effective because this plant is difficult to pull and quickly sprouts after cutting.

Host For Butterflies, Bees, Birds   Attractive to all three. Important pollen source and much more. Attracts bees, wasps and butterflies to its flowers as soon as they are open in the morning. The bees use them as principal pollen source while wasps and butterflies use them as nectar. Potential pollen and nectar sources for honey bees. In Africa honey bees collect Sida pollen voraciously and deposit it in their hives. Ceratina bees, small carpenter bees, also gather pollen for use in brood development.

Honey bees require ten essential amino acids, six out of which are present in the pollen of these Sidas, plus some non-essential amino acids. The pollen protein content is also nutritionally important.

Sida Actions and Benefits

The broad expanse of these Sida actions and benefits are completely documented in the "big book". While only titles are very dissatisfying, that was all that was possible in this short book, and they at least give you an idea of the range of Sidas actions.

Both peer-review results and traditional uses are included – I do not differentiate between them. At least one species of Sida has been studied in each category. Usually if one Sida has a positive effect, the other medicinal species should also.

Adaptogen   Allergy, Antihistamine   Animals, Disease   Arteries, Atherosclerosis   Arteries, Thrombosis   Arteries, Vasorelaxation   Ayurvedic, Aromatic   Ayurvedic, Atitikta (bitter)   Ayurvedic, Daha (burning sensation)   Ayurvedic, Hima (Cold)   Ayurvedic, Svadu-sweet in taste   Ayurvedic, Tridoshanut   Ayurvedic, Vata– Pitta diseases   Other Ayurvedic   Bladder, Cystitis   Bladder, Diuretic   Bladder, Hematuria   Bladder Problems   Bladder, Stones (calculus)   Bladder, Urinary disease   Bladder, Urinary disorders   Blood, Anti-diabetic   Blood Cleaner   Blood disorders   Blood, Diabetes mellitus   Blood, Haemolysis   Blood, Hypoglycemic   Blood pressure depressant   Blood, Stops bleeding   Blood, Thrombolytic activity   Body, Adaptogenic   Body, Alertness   Body, Anti-convulsant   Body, Antioxidant   Body, Arthritis and Osteoarthritis   Body, Chemoprotective   Body, Chills   Body, Depression   Body, Detoxification   Body, Edema   Body, Fever (Antipyretic)   Body, Gout   Body, Immuno-stimulant   Body, Immuno-supportive   Body, Inflammation   Body, Jaundice   Body, Leprosy   Body, Muscles   Body, Obesity   Body, Rheumatism   Body, Stimulant   Body, Strength   Body, Thirst

Body, Tonic   Body, Weight Change   Body, Wound healing   Brain, Myocardial injury (MI)   Brain, Neurodamage   Brain, Neurotoxicity   Brain, Other conditions   Children, Child's remedy   Catch Plant   Companion Plant   Ear and Nose Problems   Eye Problems   Fat/lipids, Increases HDL   Fat/lipids, Inhibits lipid peroxidation   Fat/lipids, Lowers cholesterol   Fat/lipids, Lowers LDL   Fat/lipids, Lowers Triglycerides   Fiber crop   Fiberglass Food, Food storage protection   Food, For humans   Food, Other than human   Food, Tea   Fuel, Heat production   GI tract, Abdominal pains   GI tract, Colic   GI tract, Constipation   GI tract, Diarrhea   GI tract, Digestive Problems   GI tract, Dysentery   GI tract, Flatulence (farts)   GI tract, Gastric disorders   GI tract, Hemorrhoids   GI tract, Laxative/Enema   GI tract, Stomach, Disorders   GI tract, Stomach, Ulcer   GI tract, Stomachic   GI tract, Tenesmus   Hair   Head, Headache   Heart, Arrhythmia   Heart, Bradycardia   Heart, Cardioprotective   Heart, myocardial infarction   Heart, Heart disease   HIV/AIDS   Insect, Anti-sida   Insects, Beneficial   Insects, Defense against   Insects, Food and Sustenance   Kidney, Nephroprotective   Kidney, Stones   Liver, Bile disorders   Liver Disorders   Liver, Hepatoprotective   Lungs, Asthma   Lungs, Bronchitis   Lungs, Cough and wheezing   Lungs, Expectorant   Lungs, Pneumonia   Lungs, Tuberculosis   Metal, Anti-corrosion   Minerals, Mineral accumulator, Chelator   Minerals, Nanoparticles   Mollusks, Molluscicide   Mouth, Demulcent   Mouth, Dental hygiene   Mouth, Inflamed   Mouth, Toothache   Nausea, Antiemetic   Nerves, CNS central nervous system depressant   Nerves, Nervous disorders   Nerves, Neurodegenerative diseases   Nerves, Paralysis   Nerves, Sciatica   Nerves, Sedative   Noise Reduction   Pain, Analgesic   Pain, Antinociceptive   Parasites, Anthelmintic   Parasitic protozoa, Malaria   Parasitic protozoa, Other   Poison, Alexertic   Poison, Neutralizes poison   Reproduction, Abortifacient   Reproduction, Anti-fertility   Reproduction, Aphrodisiac   Reproduction, Contraceptive, anti-implantation   Reproduction, During labor   Reproduction, Estrogenic activity   Reproduction, Female sexual problems   Reproduction, Leucorrhoea   Reproduction, Low or no sperm   Reproduction, Male sexual problems   Reproduction, Pregnancy   Reproduction, Uterine disorders   Sanity, Delirium   Skin, Abscess   Skin, Astringent   Skin, Boils   Skin, Cooling   Skin, Diaphoretic/Sudorific   Skin, Emollient   Skin, Rashes and Inflammation   Skin, Skin beauty   Skin, Skin disease   Skin, Sores

Skin, Lessen Perspiration   Skin, Wound healing   Sleep, Sleeping time   Soap, For Washing   Soil, Rejuvenates degraded soil Toxicity, Low/no toxicity   Toxicity, Protection from toxic metals Toxicity, Toxic to living things   Venereal Disease, Gonorrhea Venereal disease   Worms, Earthworm friendly   Other Uses

Pathogens Known to be Susceptible to Sidas

The following are the pathogens that at least one Sida species was tested against. Usually, if one Sida is effective against a pathogen, the other medicinal species should also have an effect. If it is not on this list, the pathogen has not been studied and the effects of Sida against it are unknown.

Antibacterial [Sidas have been shown to be active against the following bacteria]: Bacillus cereus   Bacillus cereus LMG 13569 Bacillus licheniformis   Bacillus megaterium   Bacillus subtilis Bacillus subtilis MTCC441   Bacillus subtitlis NCM 2439   Bacillus subtilis NCIM 2063   Bordetella bronchiseptica   Campylobacter coli   Campylobacter jejuni   Campylobacter spp.   Citrobacter freundii   Corynebacteriun diphtheriae   Enterobacter aerogenes Enterobacter aeruginosa   Enterobacter agglomerans Enterobacter cloacae   Enterococcus spp.   Enterococcus faecalis CIP 103907   Enterococcus faecalis   Escherichia coli   Escherichia coli ATCC25722   Escherichia coli MTCC 40   Escherichia coli CIP 105182   Eschorichia coli NCIM 2065   Escherichia coli NCM 2965 Escherichia coli NCTC 10418   Escherichia coli NCTC 11560 Helicobacter pylori   Kebsiella ozenae   Kebsiella pneumonia Klebsiella aerogenes   Klebsiella spp.   Listeria innocua LMG 13568 Micrococcus luteus (Sarcina lutea)   Micrococcus luteus ATCC 9341 Moraxella catarrhalis   Morganella morganii   Mycobacterium phlei   Mycobacterium abcessus   Mycobacterium abscessus Mycobacterium aurum   Mycobacterium bovis BCG Mycobacterium fortuitum   Mycobacterium smegmatis Mycobacterium tuberculosis   Neisseria catarrhalis   Neisseria gonorrhoeae   Pantoea agglomerans   Pasturella multocida Proteus mirabilis   Proteus vulgaris   Proteus vulgaris MTCC 426 Pseudomonas aeruginosa   Pseudomonas aeruginosa ATCC 27853 Pseudomonas aeruginosa DSMZ1117   Pseudomonas aeruginosa MTCC 424   Pseudomonas aeruginosa NCM 2036   Pseudomonas

cichorii   Pseudomonas fluorescence   Salmonella enterica
(Salmonella choleraesuis)   Salmonella enteritidis   Salmonella
parathyphi   Salmonella typhi   Salmonella typhimurium (typhoid)
Salmonella thyphimurium ATCC13311   Sarcina lutea (Micrococcus
luteus)   Shigella boydii   Shigella dysentariae   Shigella
dysenteriae CIP 54051   Shigella flexneri   Shigella flexneri MTCC
1457   Shigella shiga   Shigella sonnei   Staphylococcus aureas
Staphylococcus aureus MRSA   Staphylococcus aureus NCM 2010
Staphylococcus aureus ATCC25903   Staphylococcus aureus ATCC
25923   Staphylococcus aureus ATCC 53154   Staphylococcus
aureus MTCC 87   Staphylococcus aureus NCIM 2079
Staphylococcus aureus NCTC 10788 (MRSA)   Staphylococcus
aureus NCTC 11561 (MRSA)   Staphylococcus aureus SS-1VC
Staphylococcus aureus SS-2VM   Staphylococcus aureus SS-3SW
Staphylococcus aureus SS-4OM   Staphylococcus aureus SS-5BC
Staphylococcus aureus SS-6AF   Staphylococcus aureus SS-7DS
Staphylococcus carmonum carmonum LMG 13567   Staphy-
lococcus epidermidis   Staphylococcus epidermidis ATCC 12228
Staphylococcus epidermidis MTCC 2639   Streptococcus faecalis
Streptococcus mutans   Streptococcus mutans ATCC 700610
Streptococcus mutans w7,w11,w13   Streptococcus pneumoniae
Streptococcus pyogenes   Streptococcus salivarius   Streptococcus
sanguis ATCC 10556   Streptococcus sanguis w14,w18,w20
Streptococcus viridans   Vibrio cholerae   Vibrio mimicus   Vibrio
parahemolyticus   Xanthonomonas axonopodies pv. Malvacearum

Anti-Fungal [Sidas have been shown to be active against the
following Fungi:]   Alterneria Alternata   Aspergillus flavus
Aspergillus fumigates   Aspergillus niger   Aspergillus niger NCIM
1054   Aspergillus ochraceus   Candida albicans   Candida albicans
MTCC No. 183   Candida albicans ATCC 10231   Candida albicans
ATCC 2091   Candida albicans ATCC 9002   Candida albicans
ATCC 90028   Candida albicans NCIM 3102   Candida albicans
NCPF 3242   Candida albicans NCPF 3262   Candida glabrata
Candida guilliermondii   Candida guilliermondii LM 28   Candida
intermedia   Candida krusei   Candida krusei ATCC 6258
Candida krusei LM 07   Candida parapsilosis   Candida
parapsilosis ATCC 22019   Candida tropicalis   Candida tropicalis
ATCC 750   Candida tropicalis LM 25   Candida tropicalis NCPF
Candida tropicalis NCPF   Candida tropicalis NCPF 3242   Candida
tropicalis NCPF 3262   Cryptococcus neoformans   Saccharomyces

cerevisiae   Cunninghamella elegans   Dreschlera turcica
Fusarium oxysporum   Fusarium verticillioides   Microsporum
gypseum   Penicillium FCF 281   Trichoderma spp.   Rhizopus
oryzae   Saccharomyces cerevisiae   Saccharomyces cerevisiae
NCPF 3139   Saccharomyces cerevisiae NCPF 3178   Scpulariopsis
candida   Trichophyton mentagrophytes LM 103   Trichosporon
inkin   Ustilago maydis

Cancers   Cancer Treatment   Adenocarcinoma   Blood cancer
Breast cancer   Liver cancer   Colon cancer   Hepatoma   Leukemia
Lung cancer   Lung fibroblast cells   Osteosarcoma (Bone cancer)
Ovarian cancer   Preneoplastic lesions   Cancer, Other Cancer
Cancer, Cytoxic

Insects   Protozoa, and the like   Acanthoscelides obtectus-bean
weevil   Aedes aegypti   Anopheles stephensi   Culex
quinquefasciatus   Earias vittella   Plasmodium berghei
Plasmodium falciparum

Anti-Viral   Herpes simplex virus, types 1 and 2   Influenza
Polio   Sindbis   Virus, General Antiviral, Traditional

Sidas Compared to Pharmaceutical Drugs

This listing is far from complete. It is from peer-review studies that
found that experimental quantities of one particular medicinal Sida
(species and how extracted not identified) matched the
effectiveness of a pharmaceutical drug. Please do not use this
information for any health condition. The sole purpose of this
listing is to demonstrate that Sidas have medicinal constituents that
can have effects comparable to pharmaceuticals.

These studies are usually the results of experiments on test animals
(not humans). Many use one highly-concentrated constituent from
some part of some Sida plant, The concentrations are usually much
higher than you would get from a Sida extract, nevertheless much
smaller natural concentrations can have a very positive effect over

time.. Other examples below you will notice are effective as a crude extract.

Whole plant extract at 300µg/ml. was more effective than **terbinafine** to combat the pathogenic fungi. (antifungal, whole plant)

2 mg acqueous as powerful as **Fluconazole** 25 mcg. (leaf tea anti-fungal)

The same extracts at 300µg/ml showed promising activity and comparable to standard drug **griseofulvin.** (anti-fungal)

Whole plant—100 mg/kg bw--zone of inhibition (mm)-Acqueous extract 19 mm-ethanolic extract 20 mm- **streptomycin** (1mg 22.6 mm) 19.6 mm- **Ampicillin** (1 mg/ml) 34.60 mm. (antibiotic, water and ethanolic extract)

100% ethanolic extract-at 1000 mg/ml has better ZI (zone of inhibition) (22) than **gentamicin** (18).   (antibiotic, ethanolic leaf extract)

Ethanol extract antimicrobial activity 86%-MIC .96-1.8 ug/ml-- **lincomycin** antimicrobial activity 80%. lincomycin MIC 7.8-31.2 ug/ml. (antibiotic-crude ethanol extract!)

Aqueous extract at 300µg/ml was comparable to that of standard drug **norfloxacin.** (antibiotic)

Maximum inhibition was at 400mg/kg bw (83.78%). The effects were comparable with that of reference standard, **indomethacin.** (NSAID-exhibited no ulcerogenicity)

The activities of the extracts were comparable to the standard drug, **phenylbutazone.** (NSAID)

Leaf-inhibition of edema by butanolic extract is comparable to that of **phenylbutazone**. (NSAID)

400 mg/kg were very much comparable with **pentazocin** 10 mg/kg. (pain killer, water and ethanol extracts)

Polyphenol rich fractions showed good activity compared with that of standard drug **paracetamol**. (pain reliever and a fever reducer.)

In all categories treatment resulted in lower values than the standard drug **Diclofenac** 0.3 mg/kg.) (pain, inflammation, arthritis, ethanol extract)

100   mg/kg bw compared against the standard analgesic, **aminopyrine** 50 mg/kg.   (analgesic, anti-inflammatory, and antipyretic)

50% ethanolic extract has got potent antioxidant and antiinflammatory activity and the activity is comparable with the standard drug **deprenyl.** (anti-depressant, Parkinson's)

Aqueous and total aqueous extracts showed significant antihepatotoxic activity comparable to that of **silymarin.** (hepatoprotective, water extract)

Acqueous extract had better cardiotonic activity than **digoxin.** (cardiotonic, root tea)

leaves-400 mg/kg bw-extracts reduced blood glucose levels: ethanolic 30%, acqueous 54%-comparable to **tolbutamide** 40 mg/kg bw 55%. (type 2 diabetes)

....

The use of herbal medicine can be traced back to 2100 BC in ancient China at the time of Xia dynasty, and in India during the Vedic period. The first written reports are timed to 600 BC with Charaka samhita of India, and in China the same became systematic by 400 BC. The basic concept in these medicinal systems is that the disease is a manifestation of a general imbalance of the dichotomous energies that govern life as a whole and human life in particular, and they focus on medicine that can balance these energies and maintain good health.

An entire section of the Materia Medica of Ayurveda termed Rasayanas is devoted to the enhancement of the body resistance. Interestingly, a somewhat similar role is ascribed to tonics and various herbals in the Chinese and European systems of medicine. Rasayana generally means nourishing and rejuvenating drugs with multiple applications for longevity, memory enhancement, immunomodulation and adaptogenic. Various drugs listed as Rasayana have been researched and have been reported to possess pharmacological activities such as immunostimulant, tonic, neurostimulant, antiaging, antibacterial, antiviral, antiseptic, anti-rheumatic, anticancer, anti-inflammatory, adaptogenic, anti-stress etc. Several botanicals from the Rasayana category have been studied for immunomodulation and have a potential of becoming new scaffolds for safer, synergistic, cocktail immunodrugs... Bala (can be any of these three Sidas) is a root drug commonly used in Ayurveda as a general tonic and "rasayana" drug.

The drug 'Bala' (Sida) in Sanskrit is well reputed as anti-rheumatic and anti-pyretic in the Ayurvedic system of medicine and is also used for curing neurological disorders, headache, leucorrhoea, tuberculosis, diabetes, fever and uterine disorders. It is also reported to possess anti-tumor, anti-HIV, hepatoprotective, abortifacient, antimicrobial and immunostimulant properties.

About the Author

I have been a plant person most of my adult life. My wife and I started **Bountiful Gardens Seeds** in 1982, which was part of **Ecology Action of the Midpeninsula**, an organization that has been desperately trying to save the world's soil for the last 45 years, while refining a farming method (biointensive) that actually creates soil while being very productive.

We started **Bountiful Gardens** because heirloom, open-pollinated seeds were hard to come by in the 1980s, and disappearing. At the time it was not certain that these heirloom seeds would continue to be available to the general public. We offered a considerable number of varieties that otherwise would not have been available. Back then we also had a "Healing Herbs Garden Club" that really educated me in medicinals of all sorts. BG has always carried a strong section of medicinal plant seed.

For years I selected many of the varieties we carried in our catalog, which was not unlike being an Indiana Jones of the plant world. All of this has given me good experience with discovering the useful properties of a plant. It also helps to be married to a biologist who fills in any blanks. I retired as the third longest-tenured employee ever at Ecology Action after our founders.

I consider myself a personal herbalist. I do not have the intimate, extensive knowledge of hundreds of herbs that a professional herbalist would know, but rather I know very well the few plants that I need, seeking only my health, and the health of my family. Medicinal herbs and preventative medicine have been at the core of my family's health for at least 50 years. I know the plants I use very well, and when I discover a new one that is as good as Sida is, I am completely on board right away, and want to know everything about it.

The next step is a thorough and intensive research into its known benefits. So for over years I intensely scoured the internet for peer-review research on Sida, and in particular studies on Sida acuta, the species that I use. The results have exceeded my wildest expectations.

Former Lives

Walked away from two degrees at Cal Berkeley in the 60s. Spent time in the Haight-Ashbury. Lived on the margins of society - until I became a father. That changed everything. Both my son and step-daughter eventually graduated from Stanford University.

For better or worse, I am one of the people who brought personal computers into being. I am a "76er" – anyone involved before 1976 was a genuine pioneer. I worked for the People's Computer Company of digital legend, as well as running database marketing for the very first Computer Faires. Once it stopped being a crusade and became an industry I became a gardener of sorts. Having a computer background was very helpful when starting a seed company in the 1980s.

Around 1990 I created a poster, **The Vegetable Gardener's Guide** (in its third printing), that has been a perennial favorite of master gardeners and garden centers – they are grateful to have all the essential questions beginners ask right there on the wall. It is available from my website (www.bbruneau.com).

In 2004 I decided to put my enthusiasm for the French bidet into a book. As often happens with me, this book turned out to be the first book on the topic, ever! Could not find anything in print. There was nothing in the Library of Congress at the time except a note by President Thomas Jefferson on the bidet as a result of his visit to Paris in the 1700s. What a treat to write the first book on anything in 2004! I discovered everything known at the time, and went beyond by adding information from other knowledge bases, resulting in a book whose information is still very complete and current today. I hope to have it reprinted soon.

The Bidet: *Everything There is to Know From The First and Only Book on The Bidet; An Elegant Solution for Comfort, Health, Happiness, Ecology, and Economy; The Topic No One Talks About, A Device That Can Save Your Health.* It immediately became the reference on the subject. It still is commonly known in the business as the "bidet bible", because it included every thing known about the bidet, and more. Used copies, when you can find them, are going for $30 or more.

Disclaimer   (continued from inside title page)

I am not a doctor and I am not qualified to give you direct medical advice. I report research on aspects of the genus Sida, including medical research. The sources are peer-review research, and other expert sources, as well as traditional uses. I do not warrant that any claims here are true or accurate.

No health benefits in this book have been evaluated or approved by the FDA. They should not be used in place of personal judgment or medical treatment when needed, nor is anything in this book intended to diagnose, treat, cure or prevent any disease. Only your doctor can diagnose and treat disease.

None of the information in this book is intended to be taken as direct medical advice. Always consult with your medical practitioner before trying any knowledge you have learned from this book. Readers should not act upon any information provided in this book without seeking advice from a licensed physician.

I expressly disclaim all liability with respect to actions taken or not taken based on any of the contents of this book. If I provide any specific examples of medical outcomes here, please be advised that I personally do not recommend them. This book is based on another book I wrote (Sida acuta, Sida cordifolia, Sida rhombifolia, Etc.: Everything Science and Tradition Knows About the World's Best Herbal Antibiotics, Used by Millions of People Every Day, Top Ayurvedic Herbs, Protein-Rich Survival Plants, Superior Fiber, Grow Them with Your Tomatoes ISBN = 978-0-9748799-3-2) and is only my opinion based upon findings of this other book. It is for informational purposes only and not meant to be medical advice.

The information in this book is intended only for scientific exchange. It has not been approved by the United States Food and Drug Administration for publication nor does it have any official status. Information herein is from the public domain. Any copyrighted or privately owned material inadvertently included will be removed as soon as possible.

For information or concerns about the toxicity of plants, contact the local Poison Control Center in your area. A directory of these is available from The American Association of Poison Control Centers (http://www.aapcc.org/)

For more information on the genus Sida, photos of medicinal Sidas, or to purchase naturally-grown seed, see my website   (bbruneau.com).

If you buy the "big book" from my website I will include a free packet of Sida acuta seed, free postage and no tax. That is:

567 pages   809 citations   Price $30 postpaid, tax-free, free seed